I-SPY

I-SPY AT THE SCHOOL GATE
My Mum's Better Than
Your Mum

By
SAM JORDISON

HarperCollins*Publishers*
1 London Bridge Street
London SE1 9GF

www.harpercollins.co.uk

First published by HarperCollins*Publishers* 2016

10 9 8 7 6 5 4 3 2

A catalogue record of this book is available from the
British Library

ISBN 978-0-00-822071-6

Printed and bound by Bell & Bain Ltd, Glasgow

The I-SPY concept is simple. It's like the 'I spy with my little eye' game, only instead of all the tedious stuff about 'something beginning with', there are pictures and descriptions and genuine opportunities to use your sleuthing skills to discover interesting things. And laugh at them. It will greatly improve your thus far ignorant life.

At the school gates, everyone is childish. You'll see over-excitement, sexual tension, poor discipline, bad language, bullying and temper tantrums. Especially among the parents. It really is a world unto itself – with a unique fauna and its own complex set of social patterns that generally revolve around impenetrable cliques and complicated competitions. There are also interesting displays of status and costume. All of which provide a simply topping challenge for good I-SPYers!

You earn a score every time you spot something pictured in this book. It's great fun to add up your scores and know that you're doing better than your friends and family.

When your score totals over 250, you're allowed to call yourself an I-SPY Stalwart, second-class honours.

When your score totals over 500, you're a teacher's pet. Hello, darling!

If you score less than 250, you're a failure and should go straight to the back of the class.

Chief I-SPY, LONDON

Wholesomes

Many of these people will look like they've just been knitted. Others will have children ostentatiously wearing clothes they've created themselves. They'll all enjoy telling you how nice they and their friends are. They'll chat together about how much fruit their children eat. They'll be among the first to volunteer for the PTA. And they'll judge you. Hard.

I-SPYed on.. Score

at .... (30)

The Family That Is Always Late

I-SPYers who hang around for a few minutes after the morning bell will be able to spot this family performing the fast walk of shame towards the school gates. It's always nice to smile at them and stroll slowly and comfortably the other way.

I-SPYed on .... Score

at .... **(20)**

The Family That Is Always Late may be eating breakfast as they run, in which case award yourself 30 extra bonus points.

I-SPYed on .... Score

at .... **(30)**

The Family That Is Always Late may also be you. In which case subtract 40 points.

I-SPYed on .... Score

at .... **(-40)**

Hot Dad

This dad is single, and oh, look at his bulging guns and his sweet, only ever-so-slightly-damaged expression, and it wouldn't be too strange if you asked him out for a drink, would it? Oh, crikey! He's looking your way. Don't blush!

Too late.

I-SPYed on... Score

at .... (20)

The Supermum

She's always on time. She's bright and bouncy, morning
and evening. She's sweet and smiling! Her kids are
sweet and smiling! Their packed lunch is super-healthy.
She remembers your name and always has a polite word
to say. She's just lovely! You hate her the most.

I-SPYed on .... Score

at .... (10)

A Gossip Column

If you're very lucky, one morning you'll arrive at school to see a chat line in progress. Someone has heard some exciting news! Everyone else is waiting to hear it. These are the best moments. Savour them.

I-SPYed on .... Score

at .... (**40**)

If the gossip is about a teacher's love life,
score an extra 50 points!

I-SPYed on .... Score

at .... (**50**)

Amorous Couple

Every class has two parents who've had a top-secret affair that absolutely everyone knows about. You can tell who they are by the way they aren't talking to each other, the way half of the other parents aren't talking to them either and the fact that they're a constant source of discussion. It's important to befriend them both on Facebook to see how things develop and to make it easier for you to predict the day, midway through term, on which one of them will show up drunk and screaming. You can then award yourself 20 I-SPY points for your clever diligence.

I-SPYed on .... Score

at .... (20)

Witness a lovers' tiff and score 20 extra points.

I-SPYed on .... Score

at .... (20)

Chelsea Tractor

This is a large car designed for off-road countryside driving and driven by people who only actually see mud when it comes in £50 pots from Harrods and is worn in the bath.

The best time to spot these is during rush hour, when they're usually out blocking the narrow roads around school.

I-SPYed on .... Score

at .... (10)

If you see one being driven by a blonde woman angrily shouting into a phone, you can have an extra 20 points!

I-SPYed on .... Score

at .... (20)

A Boden of Mums

A Boden of mums is a group of three or more women gathered at the school gates in affluent towns wearing boldly coloured, stripy clothes.

I-SPYed on .... Score

at .... (**30**)

Some of these lovely mums may be carrying tote bags bearing messages about how much they love reading books. If they are, give yourself an extra 10 points.

I-SPYed on .... Score

at .... (**10**)

If you see someone with a book tote actually reading a book, take the maximum 80 points! This is one of the rarest sights in the UK.

I-SPYed on .... Score

at .... (**80**)

Breeders

How many children is too many? It's wrong to judge –
but it's also fun! Oh dear! Pity the poor mum pushing
a double-pram, with another child strapped above her
pregnant belly in a sling and two others starting fights all
over the school. Why won't her husband leave her alone
at night? She must be tired enough as it is.

I-SPYed on .... **Score**

at .... ⑳

Exercise Bunny

Taking exercise isn't necessarily shameful. Sometimes even respectable citizens enjoy a nice quiet jog or a dip in the swimming pool. But right-minded people do get alarmed when others start brazenly advertising their vices and turn up outside the classroom in training shoes, leggings and other such kinky items. Good I-SPYers do not enjoy knowing too much about the contours of other people's bodies.

Still, try not to get too anxious when a sporty mum or dad bounces into your personal space. The bad news is that they probably haven't had a shower yet. But the good news is that they'll enable you to collect some lovely I-SPY points.

I-SPYed on.. **Score**

at... (**25**)

Tiger Mum and Dad

Tiger parents are hard to spy at first because they appear normal, if a little earnest. But you won't have to use too many spying skills to wheedle out their identity. Soon they'll be unable to stop themselves from asking about your children's test scores and whether they attend 'many' after-school clubs, and addressing your offspring in French – just to see how well they're doing. The only thing they relish more than their own child's success is your child's failure. *Soyez prudent!*

I-SPYed on .... **Score**

at .... **(20)**

The Enemies

Did you hear what she said about her? Do you know what she only went and did? Were you there when it happened? No? Well, don't worry because no one else was either. All we know is that their hatred is as ancient and dark as the days before the sun.

You'll know the enemies are nearby because, even on hot days, ice will start forming on the end of your nose. Their special characteristics include being able to not see each other from across the playground and to roll their eyes at the mere mention of their enemy's name – roll them so far that you can only see the bloodied whites.

I-SPYed on .... Score

at .... **(25)**

Diligent spies may also see the enemies' husbands, who have no mutual animus, nodding at each other in sad, embarrassed recognition.

I-SPYed on .... Score

at .... **(10)**

The Imminent Divorce

Not all parents get along. Some can't bear to be in the same room. Which makes sleeping in the same bed all the trickier. But their loathing keeps lawyers in business and so helps to oil the cogs of one of the UK's few remaining successful industries.

You'll know who they are because the wife is always crying and checking her phone and the husband keeps getting drunk and staring at other mums' lills and hahas for far too long.

I-SPYed on .... **Score**

at .... **(30)**

The Scary Dog

He isn't, as his owners insist, a 'good boy'. He's a
bad boy. And he has his eyes on your child.

I-SPYed on .... Score

at .... ⑩

The Still-raving

They haven't slept since that 'banging' night in Turnmills in 1997 and they won't let kids ruin their fun. They're still having it large and it's great. Ignore the sadness in their eyes. Youth never dies!

You'll know who they are because they'll start bouncing in time whenever a pneumatic drill goes off nearby. And because they'll have the straightest, quietest children in the class.

I-SPYed on .... **Score**

at .... (40)

Brexit Dad

The scary thing about Brexit Dad is that he looks quite like you or me. It takes careful listening to recognise him. 'I did vote Leave...' he'll admit eventually, 'but...'

I-SPYed on .... **Score**

at .... (**20**)

Spot a Brexit Dad and a Guardianista (p.48) talking fervently and entirely failing to listen to one another.

I-SPYed on .... **Score**

at .... (**20**)

The SHOUTING Parents

Come HERE. We're LATE. DON'T DO THAT TO YOUR BROTHER. YOU LITTLE...!

You want to tell them to be nicer to their children, but you're too scared... At least they're easy to I-SPY.

I-SPYed on .... **Score**

at .... (20)

Frightened Dad

It may be the 21st century, but there are still many more mums at the school gates than dads. And as those dads who do show up will tell you, this is at once quite nice, very scary and another reason to bless the inventor of smartphones – an eternal excuse to look busy and otherwise engaged.

I-SPYed on .... Score

at .... (20)

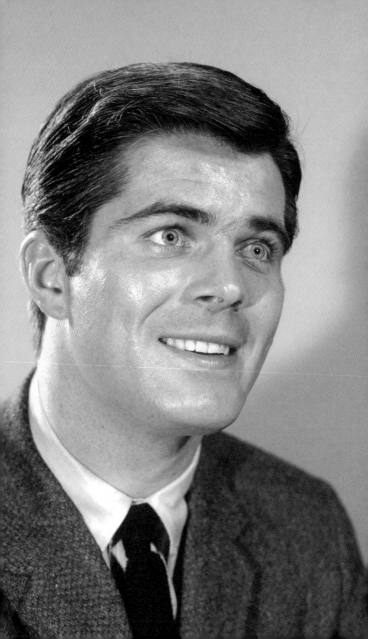

The Businessman

The businessman is hard to spot because he's always hurrying. Often his presence is marked only by the faint smell of aftershave in the air. But diligent spies will see him eventually. In the end he won't be able to resist putting in an appearance at the school gates in order to remind you that he's earning more money than you are.

I-SPYed on .... Score

at .... (**30**)

Spot the businessman hurrying into his BMW, failing to indicate and screeching off at 50 mph in a 20 mph zone.

I-SPYed on .... Score

at .... (**30**)

The Potty-mouth Mummy

She looks as fresh as a meadow in May. Her voice is as clear and shiny as cut glass. But goodness gracious, the filth that comes out of her mouth could fell trees, wilt crops and kill all the little bouncing lambs of spring.

I-SPYed on .... **Score**

at **20**

The Hippy

His trousers will be baggy, his hair will be long and his mind will be as soft and squidgy as the soap he so assiduously avoids. The hippy is mainly harmless, but you should probably report him to the authorities anyway. It's fun for them to have someone to persecute.

I-SPYed on .... **Score**

at .... (30)

The Pyjama-wearing Parents

The Pyjama-wearing Parents are rare. But also easy to spot. Because they are still wearing pyjamas.

I-SPYed on .... Score

at .... **(30)**

The Pyjama-wearing Parent is sometimes interchangeable with The Family That Is Always Late (p.6). But more often they'll arrive in plenty of time, having actively decided to show up in nightwear because that's just how they roll. But if you do see a pyjama-wearing late parent, collect another 20 points.

I-SPYed on .... Score

at .... **(20)**

The Guardianistas

The poor Guardianistas! They're right about everything, but no one else can see it. They desperately try to inveigle their opinions into every conversation at pick-up time and force you to agree with them, but it won't work. They'll start off being right about education, move on to being right about Brexit, continue being right about austerity and make a witty attempt at being right about those bloody sexist *Transformers* films.

But the more right they are, the less people want to listen. The majority of the country still persists in ignoring and defying them. And that's sad. It's hard to be so right all the time! It's a challenge and a burden, and it's small wonder that liberals sometimes come across as sanctimonious bores. They're to be pitied rather than hated. Just don't let them talk to you about Jeremy Corbyn.

I-SPYed on.. **Score**

at **20**

The New to the Area

Sometimes fresh parents arrive in the area. They anxiously try to slot their child into this new environment and do their very best to make friends with the unfamiliar faces in the playground. You can help them understand how things work by spurning and mocking them. Nobody likes outsiders! The sooner they realise this and go back to where they came from, the happier they'll be.

I-SPYed on .... **Score**

at .... (30)

Some new parents may actually be of the same social class as you and dress in similar ways. In which case the best course of action is to quickly befriend these people. That way you can successfully lay the groundwork for having a huge falling-out with them six months down the line.

I-SPYed on .... **Score**

at .... (20)

Honourable Rank of
NEW SPY

—

Awarded to

....

from

....

....

(FULL NAME AND ADDRESS HERE)

has become an acceptable citizen. This person has
demonstrated vigilance and diligence and earned
the Honourable Rank of New Spy.

First-class Honours
1000 POINTS - EXTRA MERIT

NOW ENCOURAGE YOUR FRIENDS AND NEIGHBOURS TO JOIN IN. OR ELSE.